Practice Makes Perfect

Elsa Hasch/Allsport

Brian Bahr/Getty Images

Imagine flying down a mountain at a very fast speed. You use a board to guide you. Your goal is to make a safe landing after hitting a bump and doing a flip high in the air. You have cold air blowing on your face as you glide across the snow-covered mountain.

This is what it is like to be a snowboarder.
In 1998, snowboarding became an
Olympic medal sport.

Donald Miralle/Allsport

Snowboarding is an individual sport. There are no team competitions. As snowboarders get ready for their competition, they know they must rely only on themselves when they compete. Snowboarders must be dedicated and stay focused if they expect to compete in the Olympic Games. Constant practice is very important.

Brian Bahr/Getty Images

Brian Bahr/Getty Images

Olympic snowboarding has two events. These events are the **parallel giant slalom** and the **halfpipe.** A snowboarder usually chooses only one of these events to compete in during the Olympic Games.

Zoom/Allsport

In the **parallel giant slalom** race, the snowboarder competes against both time and an opponent. First, each snowboarder races alone down the course to get a qualifying time.

Allsport UK/Allsport

Then, each snowboarder is matched up with someone to race against. The two snowboarders race against each other down two identical courses. After the race, they switch courses and race again. As they race down the hill, they try to gain speed to go really fast. The snowboarders must clear gates or flags as they board down the hill.

Zoom/Allsport

Since snowboarders rely on speed and skill to win, they must practice their movements often. There is no room for mistakes at this point. The snowboarders must stay focused and have a positive attitude to handle so much pressure.

Brian Bahr/Getty Images

The other snowboarding event is the **halfpipe.** The halfpipe is performed in a snow chute that looks like a pipe cut in half lengthwise. The snowboarders go back and forth on the pipe-like slope. They do flips, turns, and spins. Snowboarders take jumps and rise high into the air. It is fun to see how high they can soar!

Allsport

The object of the halfpipe is to do complex tricks with perfect form. The snowboarders are scored in five areas. These areas are **technique, height, rotation, landing,** and **technical merit.** The snowboarders try to get really tricky. This is how they get more points than their opponents. They jump so high that they look like they are flying!

Shaun Botterill/Allsport

Snowboarders depend on strong leg muscles to help them balance and board well. With practice, exercise, and a good diet, anyone can become a better snowboarder.

Brian Bahr/Getty Images

Surfers and skateboarders usually learn to snowboard easily. They take the skills they learned while surfing or skateboarding and use those skills when they snowboard. It is great to take something you already know and use it to learn something new. Learning new things can be fun and challenging!

Allsport UK/Allsport

The **stance,** or how you stand, on a snowboard is very important. Left foot forward is the regular stance. Right foot forward is called the **goofy foot** stance.

Brian Bahr/Getty Images

There are different boards a snowboarder can use. Snowboarders use **freestyle boards** when the snow is powdery. They are great for jumps and flips.

Shaun Botterill/Allsport

Racing and **Alpine boards** are the strongest boards. They are stiffer and firmer, and they allow a racer to go really fast. Snowboarders use these boards for speed and steep slopes. Racing and Alpine boards have hard bindings. Snowboarders who use these boards wear hard boots that are similar to ski boots.

Donald Miralle/Getty Images

Although snowboarding was developed in the United States, many countries are catching the snowboard "fever." Olympic snowboarders are risk-takers who love the challenge of this extreme sport. They are fearless!